THE BEGINNING

A very good place to start . . .

Contents

DON'T NEGOTIATE WITH
LEPRECHAUNS

A Handbook of Management Principles Which Promote
Dynamic Change and Innovation

Mark E. Carey

DON"T NEGOTIATE WITH LEPRECHAUNS
A Handbook of Management Principles Which Promote
Dynamic Organizational Change and Innovation

ISBN 0-9644654-1-8

Design and Layout
John R. Higgins
American Probation and Parole Association

Editing by the American Probation and Parole Association.

Printed in the United States of America

"Whenever a discrepancy exists between the current culture and the objectives of your change, the culture always wins."
– Daryl R. Conner
"Managing at the Speed of Change"

"The Disney culture, and maintaining it, is still my number one priority."
– Michael D. Eisner
Chairman and CEO for Disney
1996 Annual Report

"History is moving at 50 or 60 miles per hour, while a bureaucracy tends to be static."
– Andrew Young
"City and State," 1990

"There are two kinds of people who dance with elephants – the quick and the dead."
– Mark Cuban
President of MicroSolutions, Inc.

F O R W A R D !

YOU KNOW THE STORYLINE.

It is played out each day in the lives of our corporations and public agencies. A manager or CEO seeks to move the organization in a different direction only to be repelled by some seemingly invisible and perplexing force. We now know what that force is. It is the organizational culture. It seeks its own waterline. It seeks status quo. Culture is made up of certain components, which define the very nature of the organizations. Some of these components are the organization's values and beliefs, commonly performed rituals, norms, the tools and technology used, shared symbols and language, and its collective history as recalled through stories. Change, then, is often psychologically viewed as the enemy. And, nine times out of ten, the existing culture succeeds in deflecting fundamental changes.

And, there's more to the storyline. Certain individuals in an organization have an uncanny ability to come up with one creative idea after another. These ideas are usually discovered and expressed with great excitement and vision. A few weeks later, not only has the innovation been watered down or died, but so has the spirit of the innovator. Why? It usually has to do with the culture and the leadership's inability to sustain the environment which supports its most creative personnel.

Of course it goes on. *The ingredients that go into the recipe for success are at risk of being chipped away and rendered impotent without a conscious and determined mindset by the organizational leadership.* Flexibility, positive problem solving, ambiguity, vision, emphasis on outcomes, joy in the workplace, etc., together create a form of synergy in which the final product far exceeds whatever each trait could produce individually. How does an organization create and sustain such an environment? It is not something that happens by chance. It requires foresight and a persistent strategy.

This handbook was created for upper and middle managers facing similar questions and challenges. The principles offered in this book were "discovered" when, as the management team of a Community Corrections Department, we attempted to promote changes in department practice from one that emphasized punishment and accountability to one which placed the victim and community on center stage through restorative justice concepts. Restorative justice seeks to engage three customers—the victim, offender, and community—in the act of mending the harm caused by crime. Traditionally, corrections has been predominantly concerned with one customer, the offender. The victim and community have been of secondary importance. Thus, the emphasis has been on punishing and monitoring the offender. Under a restorative philosophy, correctional staff is requested to take on not only new customers, but also new roles, values, and practices. Naturally, this is upsetting to the status quo, and the clash of cultures soon becomes evident.

The principles described throughout this handbook apply to any major organizational change which threatens the existing method of operation. Fortunately, my most encouraging discovery was that most individuals embrace change when they are given the opportunity to help shape it, when leadership acts with resolve and patience, and when employees know that the organization will provide the necessary supports for that change to be a successful one for all involved.

EMPLOYEE NEEDS FOR
SUCCESSFUL CHANGE

"What you believe and think about people sets into motion the kind of organization you create."
– Percy Jackson
Digital Equipment Corporation

"The trouble with the rat race is that even if you win, you're still a rat."
– Lily Tomlin

GOT MILK?

I HAVE NO IDEA IF THIS IS CONFIRMED BY SCIENTIFIC EVIDENCE, but it appears to have experiential validity. Sometimes our bodies crave certain vitamins that we apparently lack. I have noticed, for example, that in the summertime my family consumes greater quantities of iced tea, soda, and other sweetened drinks. We drink less milk. As if our bodies are in need of calcium, we suddenly crave a glass of cold, fresh milk. The urge can be overwhelming. At other times, and with other people, it may be the sun for Vitamin D, a steak for protein, or a banana for potassium.

As managers and CEOs we sometimes presume that we know what employees want or need. We set up recognition programs only to be greeted with an apathetic response. We express with great excitement some good news and are surprised by the employees' flat reaction. We need to treat employees as well as our customers. Do we ask their opinion? Do we ask them what they need? Do we make extraordinary effort to eliminate the barriers they are experiencing to get their job done? Do we individualize our response so as to meet varied needs?

Employees are motivated by different things. For some it is a paycheck or pay raise, for others it is recognition, or career enhancement. Or it can be the opportunity to work for some higher purpose, or for diversity. The possibilities are widely varied, and our responses to them should reflect this.

When an organization needs to make fundamental and systemic changes, employees' responses will differ greatly, from enthusiastic support to overt resistance. Their ability to absorb the change will differ greatly as well. Some have personal and professional lives that are stable, others do not. Some have a higher level of dispositional ability to handle ambiguity and uncertainty. For some employees work is their highest priority, whereas for others it may be much lower on the importance chain.

Don't assume that the employees are like you. What they crave may not be what you crave. Spend time discovering what it is that they need and seek to accommodate that need. Talk to them. Really talk to them. Find out what is important to them. If they are not embracing the change quickly and enthusiastically, then maybe you don't know yet why they are working for you. For organizational change to take hold, we must find out what it takes to seep that change down to the bones, into the marrow. We must increase people's resiliency by helping them land in a spot in the organization where their own personal needs are getting met. We must offer a menu of options.

Challenge Question

Does your agency recognize that employee motives differ, and provide individual approaches to institute changes?

"We must deal not only with change but with very rapid change. And that rapid change frequently leaves people physically and emotionally traumatized."

– A. Toffler

MASLOW'S LITMUS TEST

HOW DO YOU SHOW UP FOR WORK? Do you look forward to work? What needs are met at the work setting? When we received our earthly assignments, each of us came equipped with the basic human package, which in time became largely complete with its corresponding skills and needs. The skills included verbal and writing abilities, cognitive capacity, physical coordination, etc. The basic package of needs includes those items that have varying degrees of familiarity to us: the need to be recognized, to contribute, to feel appreciated, to be cared for, to experience stimulation and growth. The danger of management is to forget or ignore these basic needs, and to treat employees like machines, expecting that they will respond to alterations in their work environment like a motor would to electrical current.

To hear how some employers describe their employees can be disheartening: slothful, selfish, incompetent, and clueless. This is rarely an accurate description of the organization's most important resource, and usually is an indication that something else is amiss. Most of us seek a work experience to find meaning and to fulfill many of our needs, even if some of those needs appear to be outwardly focused (such as to discover a vaccination for a disease). Most of us are intrinsically motivated. It is part of our basic human package. And we can be further stimulated to higher levels of motivation when our needs are met through our work experiences. We work in many ways to find meaning. We work not for a company but for a movement. We want to be inspired. Our dreams are often the first casualty of life and we want to resurrect them. All too often our jobs are too small for our spirits.

Organizational change requires something extra from employees. They are asked to dig deeper, past their anxieties and skepticism, and to trust that the outcome will be better for them. They may be asked to take on extra functions when they already have too much to do. Their level of competence at the new activity will be lower, increasing their frustration and self-doubt. Why would someone be willing to accept such agency changes under these circumstances?

Take the Maslow Litmus test. Look at American psychologist Abraham H. Maslow's list of basic human motives and ask yourself if you are giving your employees the opportunity to get these needs met in their work environment. If not, don't expect that they will be internally motivated and committed to the changes being proposed.

MOTIVATIONAL NEED	QUESTIONS TO ASK
1.Physiological (food; drink; relief of tension, pain, and discomfort)	Are your employees receiving sufficient pay and benefits to meet individual needs or to raise a family? Is the work environment a safe one?
2.Security and safety (security, stability, protection, order, and limits)	Do your employees sense company loyalty and fairness, and experience predictable rewards for performance?
3.Love and feelings of belonging (affection, relationships, and support)	Do employees have meaningful relationships in their work setting and gain a fuller sense of self-identity? Is it a place of personal support and trust?
4.Competence, prestige, and esteem (status, achievement, recognition, confidence, and mastery)	Are employees recognized for work contributions, and do they have opportunities to gain a sense of accomplishments and career advancement?
5.Self-fulfillment (self-actualization, expression of creativity)	Do employee personal values match the agency values, and do they sense that they are a part of some greater, larger purpose?
6.Curiosity and need to understand	Do your employees experience personal growth? Are they better and more knowledgeable due to their work experience? Do they develop a deeper sense of overall competence?

Challenge Question

Do you provide opportunities for employees to get their basic needs met (security, belonging, competence, self-fulfillment, curiosity, etc.)?

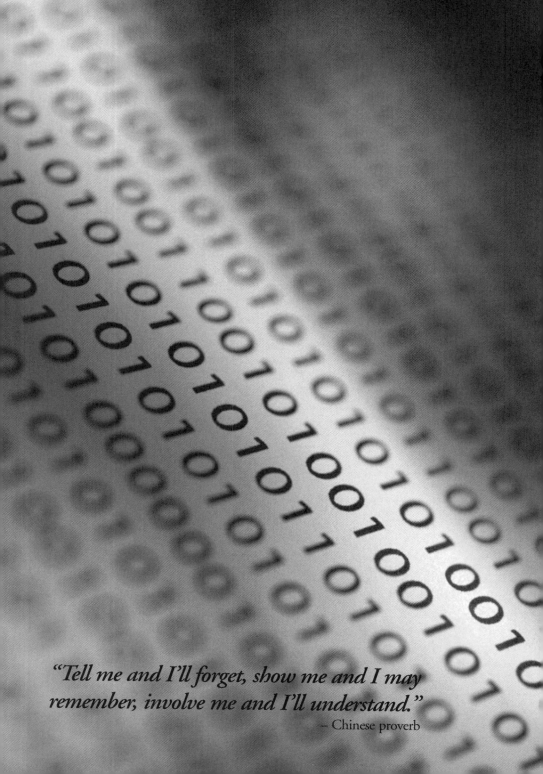

"Tell me and I'll forget, show me and I may remember, involve me and I'll understand."
— Chinese proverb

BUY-IN EQUATION

ONE OF THE MOST BASIC HUMAN NEEDS is that of autonomy—control over our own lives. In a work environment, that means our ability to influence our work process. In positive terms, this need suggests that we tend to support and view favorably those things that we helped shape; and in negative terms, we tend to oppose or view skeptically those things created without our input or that cause us to fear losing control or balance.

Allowing employees the opportunity to influence decisions takes time. It is easy for leadership to fall into the trap of thinking that it would be better or quicker for management to fulfill their role of developing policies and managing employees, and for employees to fulfill their responsibility of producing, selling, or servicing. This is false reasoning in at least two ways:

1. Decisions are better when those doing the work of producing can participate in the discussion and selection of a course of action. Where do the best ideas come from? The CEO? The customer? The personnel who are closest to the service? From outside the company altogether? The best ideas come from all of these, at different times, and under various circumstances. There isn't an idea spigot from which ideas come spraying into a bucket. But, clearly, employees who handle the job day in and day out have significant contributions to make in executive decision making because they see what works and what doesn't in their daily experiences with the customer.

2. The likelihood of successful implementation is much greater when employees who will be carrying out the new process helped shape it. The change plan becomes one of their own instead of one imposed by someone distant from them and the work that they do. The end result is allegiance, commitment, and investment to make it work.

Ed Oakley and Doug Krug in their book, *Enlightened Leadership*, describe the importance of employee buy-in and ownership in the successful application of change. One of their formulas has been aptly named the "buy-in equation." Imagine that an outside expert, or upper level management, implements a new work function, and that it is conceptually quite sound. On a scale of 1 to 10, with 10 being best, you might rate the concept as a 10. However, the buy-in will be low because the employees were not involved. So, the buy-in might get a score of 4. Multiplying the two numbers, you get a total score of 40. They point out that the agency tends to go through a four-step process which results in poor outcomes. The four steps are:

1. Identify the problem.

2. Bring in an expert.

3. Have the expert tell your employees how to do their jobs better.

4. Spend tremendous amounts of time, energy, and money trying to overcome resistance caused by step 3.

On the other hand, if the employees created a new work function without the help of an outside source, and it wasn't quite as effective as what the expert would have come up with, the concept might score an 8. But, because the buy-in would be high since the employees created it, say a 9, the total score would be 72. The chances of successful implementation are significantly higher when there is high ownership than a better work product with low employee ownership. Most agencies' attempts at change fail because they tend to concentrate on the part of the solution equation, when the best leverage gained is in the buy-in part of the equation.

The false assumption is that decision making should occur outside of employee participation because, in part, it is a better use of agency resources. Without ample buy-in, however, the agency will pay many times over for something that could have been avoided. This is even more true when the proposed changes challenge the existing agency culture, or significantly alter the work design.

Challenge Question

Are employees given regular opportunities to shape most major agency decisions?

"*The greatest discovery of my generation is that man can alter his life simply by altering his attitude of mind.*"
– William James

"*The world we have created is a product of our ways of thinking. It cannot be changed until we change those patterns of thinking.*"
– Albert Einstein

NET FORWARD ENERGY RATIO

A SIMILAR CONCEPT TO THE BUY-IN EQUATION is Oakley and Krug's Net Forward Energy Ratio. An organization is doing one of three things—advancing toward its new goals, retreating, or remaining at a standstill. It depends on where the bulk of the agency energy is. If, for example, 75 percent of the agency has accepted proposed agency changes and are focusing their energies on putting that change into practice, and 25 percent are resisting the changes, the ratio is 75 to 25, or 3 to 1. The 25 percent energy is pushing against the 75 percent, causing more limited advancement.

By getting another 15 percent of the agency to commit their energies toward support of the changes, the ratio improves to 90 percent supporting and 10 percent resisting, or a 9 to 1 ratio. Hence, small improvements make a big difference.

One of the ways Oakley and Krug suggest moving human resource energy toward the new goals is by implementing a "DNA" approach. DNA uses a positive, reinforcing technique by encouraging the desired behavior and extinguishing the undesired behavior. The model includes:

D– Decide what behavior you want more of

N – Notice it (as opposed to behavior we don't want)

A – Acknowledge or appreciate it

We tend to repeat those behaviors for which we are acknowledged, those from which we receive some benefit—particularly when it meets one of our core human needs. This positive reinforcement technique can improve the net forward energy ratio. The affirmation and acknowledgement can come in many ways. Usually the most effective are those that are visible, public, and individualized for the employee—and thereby more meaningful.

Challenge Question

Is desired employee behavior recognized and acknowledged in small ways on a day-to-day basis?

"Genius begins great works; labor alone finishes them."
– Joseph Joubert

"The final test of a leader is that he leaves behind in other people the convictions and the will to carry on."
– Walter Lippmann

GO FOR THE TUXEDO LOOK

SINCE HILLARY CLINTON POPULARIZED THE AFRICAN PROVERB, "It takes a whole village to raise a child," many refinements of that statement have been formed. One that fits for corporations is that it takes a whole group of employees to raise an idea. There are idea generators, there are sponsors, there are those who refine the idea, yet others who produce it, and finally someone who may evaluate its effectiveness. A good sponsor knows a great idea when he/she sees one. A good innovator cares simply that his or her idea is implemented, not who gets the accolades. And the list goes on. No single person deserves the full credit. The praise should be shared. Too often, it is upper level management that is widely recognized as solely responsible. Not only is this rarely accurate, it results in a lost opportunity.

One of our most basic human needs is to be recognized and appreciated. We get this need met in various settings—home, work, church, synagogue, masque, recreation, hobby, volunteer work, etc. People who put in 40, 50, or 60 hours a week at work are contributing the bulk of their waking adult life in one setting: the job. For many, if not most, recognition, belonging, esteem, and fulfillment needs are, at least in part, met through the work experience. When we are recognized, the tendency is to want to do more. We are motivated. Do we catch people doing things right? By concentrating on people's strengths we set them up to succeed.

People dress up for parties, and social gatherings. At formal affairs, partygoers come dressed in gowns and tuxedos. They want to look their best, to be seen in the best light. Every time you single out an employee for praise, you dress that employee in a tuxedo. And the more employees dressed in tuxedos and gowns, the more festive and energetic the environment. There is plenty of room for sharing recognition, and in spreading the good will that come from it.

?????? Challenge Question

Are individual employees recognized for their accomplishments in the presence of their peers?

"We do not take humor seriously enough."
– Konrad Lorenz

"A revolution for change in society must be a joyful revolution. No whipping and grim looks. It must be a party so others will want to join in."
– Author unknown

"Sometimes a laugh is the only weapon we have."
– Roger Rabbit

"The prime requisite for achievement of any aim, including quality, is joy in work."
– Deming

"A merry heart doeth good like a medicine; but a broken spirit makes one sick."
– Proverbs 17:22

"…when the laughter dies, it's an early warning that life is ebbing from the enterprise."
– Paul Hawken, best selling author

THE ROLE OF JOY

THE PROTESTANT "WORK ETHIC" IS DRIVEN BY THE NOTION THAT ALL WORK GLORIFIES GOD, and therefore should be done with all of your heart, mind, soul, and strength. We were made to work. But joy —in the workplace? That sounds so touchy-feely. Yet, it is precisely a key ingredient to an energetic and healthy work environment. Work does not need to be drudgery. In fact, work can be a source of great mental and emotional satisfaction that produces competence, self-esteem, and joy. Perhaps you've heard the quote attributed to Confucius: "Choose a job you love and you will never have to work a day in your life." Humor and fun in the workplace actually increase the creativity. We attack our work with increased vigor. They also allow us to put things in perspective.

When I think of the major conflicts in my workplace over the years, I remember disturbances over someone changing the order of names on the mailboxes, whether we should allow employees to solicit their children's school fund-raising products at the office, and whether to allow a casual dress day. We spent an inordinate amount of time on these matters as if they were crucial to our agency mission. How important would those matters be if there were an overlay of joy in the workplace? Humor puts these things in perspective. So does death. My quick test is when you are on your deathbed, will you look back on this matter as important? Will you have any regrets over what the decision was? If not, let's get on with the matters at hand.

We know that laughter actually produces a chemical reaction in our bodies. It causes a reverberation of our neural circuits, a chemical and electrical impulse, a stimulation of the pituitary gland, and the release of endorphins. These endorphins are the same chemical substance that gives you a sense of well being after vigorous exercise. It even has a molecular structure similar to that of morphine and provides the same type of pain relief. It causes the heart rate to drop, promotes relaxation and sleep, helps reduce blood pressure, and stimulates the immune system which increases resistance to disease. In other words, humor is good for us. It reduces our stress. And when our stress is reduced, we have more ability to absorb change in our lives. We have more resilience, which is a key ingredient to sustaining major organizational cultural change. A number of studies have also discovered that humor in the workplace has its benefits—improved productivity, better decisions, less anxiety and depression, and improved creativity.

Perhaps that is why having a sense of humor is identified by so many people in surveys as a primary personality trait sought in key people in their lives, whether that be a leader or someone in a personal relationship. Do you want to work for someone who is always serious, who has a grim look on his/her face, someone in front of whom you are unsure whether you are safe in letting your hair down? Of what kind of agency do you want to be a part? One that feels like drudgery, or one that is lively and upbeat? This is not about practical jokes and ha ha pranksters. This is about seeing the humorous side of things, about taking ourselves less seriously without taking the job or others lightly. The job can be hard. Life can be hard. Why make it any harder? We should be happy. It is, after all, a choice!

Challenge Question

Is work a fun place to be?

21

"A fanatic is one who can't change his mind and won't change the subject."

Sir Winston Churchill

THERE'S ONE IN EVERY CROWD— *THANK GOD!*

IN NEARLY EVERY AGENCY, THERE IS ONE. CEOs and managers aren't sure if they should be thankful or curse. But if an organization wants to push the envelop, to break out of a mold and into one that produces a better product or service, then at least one is needed. The "one" is the eccentric but brilliant employee who thinks outside the lines. It's that employee who is able, and seemingly eager, to point out when the emperor has no clothes on. Just when things seem to be flowing, when work is comfortable, the "one" throws a wrench into the machinery causing a momentary shutdown or delay as others attempt to defend what exists. They are not naysayers for the sake of naysaying. They are keen observers who are constantly questioning why and why not. Usually, these individuals are called mavericks. Usually, they are highly creative and visionary. Usually they are despised by others.

It is precisely these individuals who are needed in creative organizations. They think beyond convention, and sometimes teeter on the absurd. They tend not to abide by standard social norms, meaning that they irritate others. They may lack social skills, or not appear to care about how others are affected by their actions or words. They are driven by an individual set of needs or motivations. They may not see the immediate, practical reasons why their ideas cannot be implemented. With some fine tuning, those reasons can often be overcome, but only if members of an organization are willing to be tolerant and examine a concept on its own merit as opposed to the approach of the idea generator.

An "organization" implies a living thing: a delicate balance of innovation and maintenance, management and leadership, chaos within structure, freedom within responsibility. Without one, there cannot be the other. We live in a world where the extremes help create balance. Without evil, would there be good? Without pain, can there be joy? We have left brain and right brain characteristics. We have the ying and the yang, opportunities and threats.

The agency maverick will be rendered powerless by an organizational culture unless conscious efforts are made to protect and support him or her. This can be difficult to do. What does a CEO do when the individual violates agency norms in their zeal to push a product or make a point? Should there be different standards for different employees? Should there be favored employees who are "untouchable?" Agency leadership will need to devise ways to hold individual behaviors to some standard, while not stifling the maverick's most valuable traits. In some cases, this means creating some insulation from overly abrasive encounters. It might include messages of support for the employee's action, but nonsupport for the means. It also helps to be up front with others about your intentions. Tell them that you will tolerate a little extra from these types of employees because of the value they add to the agency. It is the unspoken words that carry inordinate and divisive influence. Once it is disclosed, its power melts away.

Challenge Question

Are eccentric, creative mavericks supported and protected by management?

23

CHANGE TECHNIQUES

"Illumination without application leads to frustration."

I GUARANTEE IT

HOW MANY TIMES AT A BASEBALL GAME DO YOU SEE THIS? Your team is staging a rally in the middle of the game, the sixth inning. They load the bases. The crowd starts to stomp its feet, and wave homer hankies and pennants. The team's best and most powerful hitter is at the plate. Three pitches later, he strikes out to end the inning. The crowd grows quiet and the anticipation is gone. It is gone through each remaining inning as well, and the team loses.

How does this happen? We get our hopes up, only to suffer a setback and the momentum is lost, seemingly forever. The road to organizational change is full of pitfalls. It's easy to get derailed and hard to keep on track. Building up momentum is critical to a sustained change effort. Nothing works as well as success. It perpetuates the desire to repeat it. It leaves us wanting for more.

Starting small is usually the prudent course of action. Small successes that are assured are far better than trying to accomplish the full-scale change all at once. And many small, individual gains add up to a large gain, and they are easier to guarantee.

By now, almost everyone is familiar with the Men's Wearhouse commercial, where the spokesperson claims, "I guarantee it!" We all want to be a part of a winning experience. We want to know that our efforts are worthwhile and that we contributed to something that is valued by others. By starting with small, guaranteed successes we can build up employee desire and commitment to sustain the change effort until the vision is ultimately reached. If successful implementation of a particular strategy is crucial to your change goals, don't gamble it all on an effort that is risky. Make sure your smaller strategies are successful first. Agency confidence can withstand failed efforts when it has a strong, collective esteem. Maintain that confidence even when failure occurs by guaranteeing other successes.

Group esteem is largely based on a collective sense of competence and efficacy. It allows us to project into the future with optimism and expectancy. We fulfill our own prophecy by taking steps consistent with our expectations, thereby further fueling our feelings of mastery and accomplishment.

Challenge Question

Are major change processes started with efforts that are guaranteed successes?

"Luck is a matter of preparation meeting opportunity."

STAR SEARCH

How many times have you experienced a situation like this? You suggest something to your boss, your spouse, or a colleague. The suggestion is given scant attention. You might get a grunt or a dismissive comment. Moments or days later, someone else suggests the same thing, and it gets an enthusiastic response. As aggravating as this feels, there is usually a good explanation for it.

We are all influenced by different sorts of people. Some of us try to please those we befriend, others those in power, others those we respect. Whatever the reason, we respond more favorably to certain people. An organizational change process cannot succeed if it doesn't have ample sponsors who possess influence over others. And these sponsors need to differ depending on who is targeted as a stakeholder in that change effort.

This is not a foreign concept. Corporations and elected legislative bodies do it all the time. Television advertisers seek celebrities who have admiring fans or possess a good image for the product line. Who are the "stars" that you will use to give credibility to your process? It is not realistic for the CEO to be the only "star." It is unusual for one person to have sufficient characteristics (such as charisma, power, humanness, position, and humor) to influence a whole organization. Create a star list and solicit their open and verbal support for your change. If possible, get them personally involved.

Challenge Question

Are respected figures recruited for support of major change events?

29

"If you want to change people's behavior, stop telling them what to do, and start telling them who they are."

NUDGE
AND FUDGE

CHANGE IS NEARLY ALWAYS A STRUGGLE FOR PEOPLE. This struggle is more pronounced when existing employee workload is high. Doing things differently or doing different things takes energy and different types of energy (mental, physical, emotional, etc.). It will naturally create a period of incompetence. Employees need to absorb the new conceptual framework or work process. Actual work effectiveness and efficiency will suffer. Time will be consumed in the expression of anxiety, frustration, or perhaps excitement. The willingness to embrace change, and all its resulting short term costs, is directly proportionate to the amount of brain time available.

It takes a certain amount of brain time to complete existing work expectations. Change adds pressure to employee processing, potentially causing emotional or mental overload. When employees sense an overload coming, they either shut down or resist that which could propel them past their perceived ability to absorb the change (i.e., flight or fight). Pushing for change without addressing this factor leads to an unsuccessful experience for all involved, often leading to blame and criticism.

Managers have choices to make in these situations when employees are already overworked. It is helpful to relieve them of their anxiety about just getting more responsibilities piled on top of existing work in the name of change. One way is to announce that new expectations will not be added until something is taken off their work platter. Another way is to adopt a *nudge and fudge* strategy.

Nudge and fudge contains two key motivational elements. Its implementation avoids a top-down, authoritarian approach. *Nudge* involves allowing the employee to decide what work functions no longer are core to the agency mission or outcomes. Management staff need to clearly articulate what is desired, through a compelling vision or mission statement, a set of key principles, and bottom line outcomes. In other words, the "what" is defined in colorful and simple terms, and the "how" is left up to the employee. Over time, the employee will prioritize what is important in this new world, and what is just wasted effort. For too many years, management has been trying to tell employees what to do when they should have been helping them identify who they are. Once they know who they are, and what the desired outcome is, the "how to do" will come naturally.

Nudging is easier to accomplish when accompanied by the *Fudge* principle. Fudge is the lining up of the reward and recognition system with the desired changes and outcomes. It is all too common for agencies to unveil a new direction or product to their employees and expect that a compelling vision alone will get them there. For many employees, a clear vision is all they need to enthusiastically retool their thinking and actions. But for most, an incentive is needed for an extra push. If the reward mechanisms have not been revised after the change is announced, the agency will not reach its goals.

Rewards come in many forms, and often those intangible ones become most important. Which people are recognized as the high achievers in the agency? Who receives the attention of the CEO? Who is publicly praised, and for what?

Challenge Question

Do employee reward mechanisms line up with new, desired agency directions?

31

"An era can be said to end when its basic illusions are exhausted."

Arthur Miller, playwright

LEARNING FROM THE COCKROACH

AN ORGANIZATION UNDER AN ADAPTIVE CHANGE PROCESS DEALS WITH MULTIPLE GENERATIONS OF EMPLOYEES. Some of these employees may have been around from the inception of the agency, others might be second generation, and yet others are fresh recruits. In order for a change process to be successful, to have evolutionary significance, it must have an impact on its reproductive system.

In evolutionary terms, some organisms which are resistive to change within themselves and which are intransigent toward the environment as a species are an evolutionary success. That is, they win the war of attrition with the environment and outlast forces of environmental change. They keep on reproducing their form of organism. This describes the shark and the cockroach. Throughout the history of evolutionary change, these species have changed remarkably little. They are basically of the same form as their early ancestors.

Agencies full of sharks or cockroaches are not adapting to their external environment, and they have found a way to resist its influence. Sometimes, the most effective way to produce change is to alter the gene pool. New recruits with a mindset consistent with the new organizational direction will begin to erode at this resistant strain of status quo culture. This requires a change in how the agency recruits, conducts interviews, sets qualifications, and orients/trains. In other words, it requires a conscious decision. It doesn't just happen. Agency leadership needs to infuse the organization with, and maintain supports for, the precise type of employee it needs in order to sustain the change effort. The bottom line is that motivation for change increases when the work experience reflects the personal values of the employees. If that match is not present, systemic change will be nearly impossible.

Challenge Question

Is significant effort placed on hiring and molding new employees whose attributes and traits are consistent with the new agency vision?

33

"The real voyage of discovery is not in seeking new lands, but in seeing with new eyes."
Marcel Proust

"How do you eat an elephant?
One bite at a time."

"Lasting improvement does not take place by pronouncements or official programs. Change takes place slowly inside each of us and by the choices we think through in quiet wakeful moments lying in bed just before dawn."
Peter Block, *The Empowered Manager*

PLANT, WATER, AND WAIT

OUR MINDSETS ARE VICTIMS OF A FORM OF MCDONALDISM. Everything is expected in instant fashion: instant coffee, speedy printing, 30-second hamburgers, overnight delivery, instant electronic communication through the Internet, and instant international faxes. We have grown accustomed to getting what we want in a flash. And if we don't we demand accountability.

We are entering the Era of Warp-Speed Change. Even though we may surround ourselves with nimble people who can respond quickly to the changing environment, we still need time to allow changes to be assimilated within our thoughts and actions. Consider how long it took households and businesses to convince themselves of the value of computers, or to recycle, or to accept self-service gas stations.

Sometimes, an idea is too radical of a change for some people to even contemplate. To suggest it in its full and final form would likely result in the idea being thrown out without serious consideration. An effective technique is to put a tamer version of the idea out, without a firm commitment to implement it. "What about this?" "Here's something to think about." "I'm not ready to support this yet, but this intrigues me…What do you think?" Or you can sponsor a brown bag luncheon to explore an idea, as opposed to establishing some implementation task force. Another way is to sponsor some training on the concept as a means of informing agency personnel of what is being done elsewhere, to get them thinking, "Why not us too?"

By not attaching an immediate commitment to the idea, you take away people's tendency to attack it out of fear. They don't need to defend against something that is just talk. In time, that seed can begin to germinate. By carefully seeding related concepts, that idea can eventually take root. Over time, the full idea will unfold, when it is less threatening because people have moved closer to its acceptance. This technique works well when there is not a compelling need to do something immediately (i.e., a crisis), but rather an opportunity that could be useful sometime in the future.

Challenge Question

Are employees, stakeholders, and customers given more time to adapt to those ideas that are more threatening?

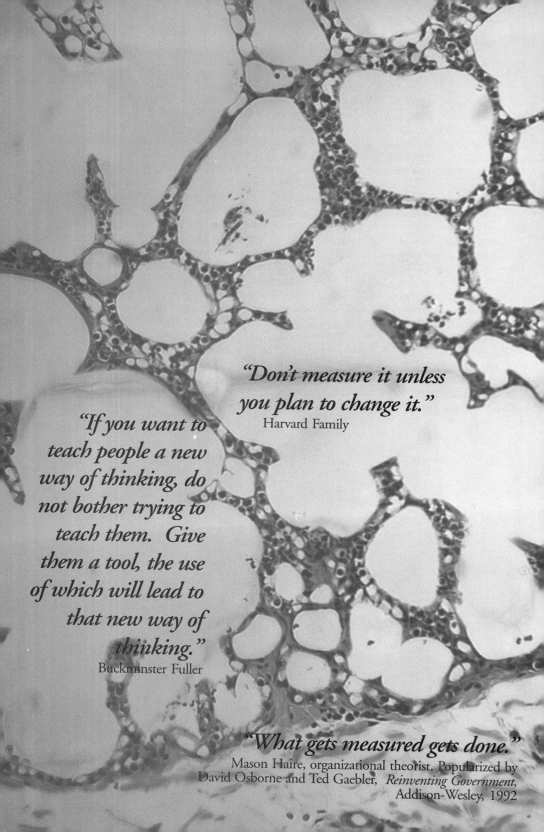

"Don't measure it unless you plan to change it."
Harvard Family

"If you want to teach people a new way of thinking, do not bother trying to teach them. Give them a tool, the use of which will lead to that new way of thinking."
Buckminster Fuller

"What gets measured gets done."
Mason Haire, organizational theorist. Popularized by David Osborne and Ted Gaebler, *Reinventing Government*, Addison-Wesley, 1992

WHAT YOU SEE IS
WHAT YOU GET

WE TEND TO BE VISUAL PEOPLE. We think in pictures, we dream in images, we put words and concepts on paper. Even our language bears this out, as evidenced by the multitude of phrases that reflect the importance of visual images: "picture this," "what you see is what you get," "I'll see you later," "a picture is worth a thousand words," "see what I mean?" "draw me a picture," "I'll believe it when I see it," and so on. And memorization techniques use bizarre and colorful mental imagery to help us remember names, numbers, words, and events. Symbols are pictures with meaning attached. Symbols engage the whole brain, right and left, conscious and unconscious.

Perhaps that is what made 3M's "sticky" notes so popular. Yellow sticky notes are everywhere. They remind us what to do, give others instructions, and provide a communication vehicle. They are visual reminders. For some, they take the place of proverbial writing on their hands in pen.

If you want to engage in an organizational change process, what visual means are you using? One of the most important is outcome measures. These measures, when tied directly to the agency mission and visually displayed, cut to the chase of what's ultimately important to the agency. If it's profits, all can see the results. If it's customer satisfaction, all can see it. If it's cost avoidance, all can see it. The likelihood of higher levels of agency performance will vastly improve when the mission is crystal clear and well communicated, when the measures tie directly to the mission-related goals, and when those outcome measures are visibly made available to all employees who play a part in making that mission and measure happen. How visible and available are your mission measures? Are they distributed widely? Are they discussed frequently? Are they posted on the walls commonly passed by employees? If you want outcomes, be visible.

Challenge Question

Do outcome measures clearly line up with desired agency direction, and are they visible to all who are responsible for the outcomes?

"Those who cannot remember the past are condemned to repeat it."

"It is not so much the articulation of goals about what an institution should be doing that creates new practice. It's the imagery that creates the understanding, the compelling moral necessity that the new way is right...Thus, if I were to give off-the-cuff advice to anyone trying to institute change, I would say, 'How clear is the metaphor? How is that understood? How much energy are you devoting to it?'"

Warren Bennis

A PICTURE SPEAKS THE ONLY WORD

IN THE PREVIOUS CHAPTER we discussed the importance of using visual representation with outcome measures. Though these are vitally important, they are not nearly as powerful a communication medium as are metaphors and imagery.

When you listen to a speaker on a particular topic and reflect on that speech days later, what do you remember? Do you recall the six main points? Or do you remember the story, which the speaker used to illustrate the point? It's the story that sticks in our mind. Our lives are full of stories—most, but not all, of which are our own. They provide a living context to beliefs, principles, and facts. They are the lines, which hold together the connecting dots for us.

Imagery is powerful. It provides us with a moral or a message while giving us the freedom to color it as our experience allows. Many versions of the same story may exist, but usually the bottom line message is the same. We can individualize it, remember it, and pull it out of recall at will. How often can we do that with pieces of information we are asked to remember?

When an organization wants to sustain a certain collective mindset in the agency, little will unite the will and desire of a group of people as much as imagery. For many, the powerful and moving Vietnam Memorial in Washington D.C. does that for those who lived through that war. For others it is remembering the scene of throngs of people gathered with Martin Luther King as he delivered his "I Have a Dream" speech. The stories about Rosa Parks, Watergate, the Challenger explosion, Lou Gherig, or Mother Theresa conjure up vivid images of a powerful message for a whole country. Each organization has a story to tell. That story, when communicated with imagery, perpetuates a piece of the organizational culture that can stand up through the most trying times. What is your agency's story? Does it provoke a visual image? What is the message? How often do you repeat it or refer to it?

Challenge Question

Does the agency have stories and symbols which powerfully communicate the company's purpose and expectations of all personnel?

LEADERSHIP ROLE IN CHANGE

"Character is following through on something long after the excitement is past."
Cabot (paraphrased)

"Character is doing something right, when no one is looking."

"Habit is habit, and not to be flung out of the window by any man, but coaxed downstairs a step at a time."
Mark Twain

DO THE WAVE

CREATING SYSTEMIC ORGANIZATIONAL CHANGE IS NOT EASY. It requires a long-term outlook, recognition that it is a journey and not a picnic. It requires persistence. It requires preparation much like planning or running a marathon.

Unlike a 100-yard dash, running a marathon takes stamina. Runners need to pace themselves. Inevitably, the marathoner will "hit a wall" whereby the pain becomes overwhelming. The temptation is to quit, or at least slow to a walk. Of course, the better marathon runners are able to recognize this psychological and physical state and push past it. Once past, they commonly experience a "second or third wind" whereby they find running easier. Often, the runner will experience a number of these walls, and has learned to expect them and prepare for them.

By its very definition, organizational culture seeks to maintain its current status. Pushing for systemwide change will create pain and anxiety. The CEO and management staff should expect to bump up against repeated psychological walls. The temptation is to give in, to accept whatever gains were made, and to forfeit the fuller, more comprehensive plan. Overcompromising is common. Or, worse, is to lack persistence. Employees need to know how serious administration is in making the change happen. Does the CEO grow tired and back off, or does she/he gather more resolve and speak/act more passionately about the changes? Is this a passing fad or is it treated like a crisis whereby all is put on the line for sake of the change? *The failure to view the change process as the number one commitment is to predict its doom.* The commitment must be visible and must stand up to inevitable adversity. Does management staff act and talk differently? Are the organizational structures changed to line up with the desired product, service, or process changes? Are the reward mechanisms changed? All of these actions will create anxiety. Some resistance will appear insurmountable. These times, as in the marathon, will test the resolve of the agency leadership to finish the race. There is no substitute for sheer determination.

I was reminded of this lesson by my son Ben when I took him to a ballgame. It was part of Minnesota Twin Kirby Puckett's retirement weekend. Accompanying my son were two of his best friends, also sixth graders. As was common this season, the Twins were losing. One of my son's friends wanted to get some excitement going, so he talked his buddies into attempting to start The Wave. First, they kindly tapped on their neighbors' shoulders and requested their help. They got lukewarm responses. Then they started yelling at the spectators around them. Once again, only a flat reaction, with one person muttering, "I hate the wave." They attempted it, and got maybe five people to cooperate. But, they didn't stop there. They got out of their seats and stood in front of the section and yelled as loud as they could that they wanted their help. They pointed at the rows of people that were to start the wave and counted, "One, two, three, GO!" Maybe twenty people, and then it died a quick death.

They returned to their seats, and I was thankful that this experiment was over. Thirty seconds later, they were on to a new strategy. They took some paper and made signs, and with each one holding one sign, they stood in front of the section with the words loudly exclaiming Wave, The, Do. Then, they ran to the next section and held the signs. They returned to their own section, and again counted, "one, two, three, Go!" Only this time The Wave started weakly and as it moved across to the next section it grew in number and noise. By the time it reached the opposite side of the stadium the cacophony was deafening. The three boys scrambled back to their seats and watched what they started. For five minutes straight, the wave moved across the stadium. And, whether by luck or inspiration, the Twins staged a rally at that moment, and eventually won the game.

You could see the glee in the boys' eyes. And, if you looked closely you could see my pride as well. They had moved a mountain of people. One of the boys turned to me and said, "Look at this! Three sixth-grade boys made 35,000 do the wave. Are we great or what!" Yes, they were great. They taught me a valuable lesson. We must be persistent if we want success. Multiple failed attempts cause easy discouragement. Adversity is to be expected. Do you have the greater resolve than those around you? After all, the sixth graders did it.

Challenge Question

Does the leadership have long-lasting stamina to outlast existing remnants of culture that resist change?

"Never go to bed mad. Stay up and fight."
– Phyllis Diller

"One doesn't discover new lands without consenting to lose sight of the shore for a very long time."
– Andre Gide
"The Counterfeiters," 1925

RIDING THE ARK WITH ZEN

MOST OF THE CHANGE PROCESS CAN BE PLANNED, SHAPED, AND GUIDED. It need not feel as though the agency is being whipsawed to and fro. If managed properly, it can be a rewarding and successful experience. However, there are times when guiding feels impossible, and attempts quite futile.

When Noah was called by God to build the ark, he responded. He followed the instructions carefully, and built an ideal model to sustain the coming torrents. He was prepared. However, when the rains came and the water rose, he was at the mercy of the storm's wrath. He couldn't force the animals to come on board—they had to be led. The storm's forces were fierce and terrible and Noah's power over it was limited. Can you imagine Noah putting a sail or rudder on the ark with the belief that he could navigate or control the forces around him? He didn't try to contain or oppose the forces but he rode on top of them rolling with them, until they ultimately subsided. He acted Zen-like.

When the change process first takes hold, it can feel like a stormy, unpredictable, and sometimes terrifying ride. Attempts at controlling the storm at this time leave leadership embattled and no closer to find calm waters. When you have control, exercise your influence. When you don't, enjoy the ride and wait it out. Patience and persistence will eventually render the storm impotent and irrelevant.

Challenge Question

Does leadership understand the art of channeling energy rather than directly fighting it?

THE "LITTLE IS BIG" RULE

As A YOUNGSTER, it had always fascinated me to listen to media commentators after a major speech by the president or some other world leader. Sometimes I was not sure that I heard the same speech. Commentators would expound on how the leader looked, whether he or she was tired, whether there was much passion in the voice, what he or she did not say, why certain words or phrases were used over others. It was not until many years later, that I realized what was happening. Leaders need to carefully construct what they say, how they say it, where it is said, and when it is said. Many thoughts are left unexpressed, some of which are difficult to disguise. This causes the viewers to wonder if the words are sincere, and whether the leader's actions behind the scenes match the words. Viewers have to look for every cue possible to determine the full message.

CEOs and management staff are no different. When a manager is describing a new directive, or agency policy shift, employees want to know whether the manager is in agreement with the change and, if so, how strongly they feel about it. When a CEO walks through an office setting, people notice who they look at and whom they don't, with whom they stop to chat, and whether they listen intently or are going through the motions. In fact, it is through these informal, spontaneous interactions that the employees get a true picture of how the agency leadership thinks about them, the product, the future of the company, etc. This is how the "little is big" rule works. The little, unscripted actions of the leadership tell the real story to the employee.

The leadership should be well aware of this factor, and take advantage of it to deliver important messages. If the agency is seeking to make a major change, the CEO can express a strong statement by simply going out of his/her way to recognize someone whose actions line up with the agency change. Everyone takes notice, and the individual employee is reinforced for the behavior. Is the CEO doing anything different since the change was implemented? How does the CEO give out his/her message in the little things?

Challenge Question

Is the leadership conscious of the little, spontaneous ways in which it communicates messages to employees?

47

"It is not the strongest of the species that survive, nor the most intelligent, but the ones most responsive to change."
– Charles Darwin

SEEK THE NIMBLE

THE LABOR MARKET IS IN CONSTANT FLUCTUATION. At times, employees with certain skills are in high demand. Eventually, training and placement processes catch up and there is a glut of that kind of employee available. Labor shortages and excess wax and wane. One thing, however, about the marketplace has not changed for many years, and likely will not for the foreseeable future as we move from the Information Age into the Era of Warp Speed: the need for flexible employees.

Skills can be learned, experience gained, and expertise developed over time. However, a character trait of flexibility, one of the most precious and sought after in today's employee, is much harder to acquire. Why is this trait so valuable? For an agency to be responsive in a constantly changing environment, it must be vigilant to fluctuating conditions, opportunities, and threats, and be willing to move quickly. Delays in response can be costly both in lost opportunities and in risk to market share. Long, drawn-out analysis and widespread contemplation are relics of the past. Only the dynamic survive. And the road to dynamism is paved with nimble people.

Nimble people aren't stuck in one way of doing something. They understand that they can take many paths, some of which may end up being shorter or less steep. They are confident in their competence, but are not overly confident of their own ability to know which path is best at all times and in every situation. They are open minded, and posses a "can-do" attitude. They don't see the world as black and white, but as an adventure during which most things are yet to be discovered.

When you hire, do you look for those employees who are flexible or those with the proper skills or experience? How do you discover this trait of flexibility in the hiring process?

?? ?? ??
Challenge Question

Does the agency consciously seek to hire flexible personnel?

49

"As always, victory finds a hundred fathers but defeat is an orphan."
– Count Galeazzo Ciano
"The Ciano Diaries 1939-1943"

THE LITTLE RED HEN PRINCIPLE

You may recall the childhood story of the Little Red Hen who asked the farm animals if they would be willing to help her make bread. Of course, no one was interested in gathering or grinding the wheat, or in kneading the dough, or in baking the bread. Once it was baking, however, and the rich aroma of the fresh bread wafted through the air, the animals were more than willing, even eager, to help the Little Red Hen eat the bread.

Sometimes, we suffer from "blind spots," a lack of vision or imagination, an apparent inability to see a product down the line, to see how actions connected together will eventually produce something of great value. Once that end result can be seen or experienced, we become eager to be a part of it. A form of jostling occurs where everyone wants some credit for their part in making the product come to life.

What we can learn from the Little Red Hen is that people need to be able to see how the dots are connected. They need to understand what the final product will look like and how it is an improvement over whatever existed before it. They need to understand how their role will play a valuable part in its finished product. The more vivid an image we create, the more we can expect that others will be able to see ahead to the end result and be motivated to do their part in making it happen. Rarely does abstraction propel people to action. People need a graphic visual image that evokes their imagination.

Challenge Question

Is the agency vision communicated in ways that enable employees to imagine what it will look like when reached?

"It is much easier to be critical than correct."

80/20 RULE

HUMAN NATURE IS NOT A SECRET. We have centuries of experience and introspective observation. We know that we respond favorably to affection. We need to be recognized and appreciated. We need to feel safe. We need to belong and to be cared for, we need diversity, we are afraid of that which we do not know, we tend to support those things we were involved in creating, and resist those in which we had no part. It is the same human nature that we bring to the work setting. Given this, some things are predictable. One of them is that when an organization studies an issue and makes a reasonable decision to make a change in response to that study, not everybody will support that change. Usually, employees fall into one of three camps: enthusiastic or general support, neutral acceptance (i.e., will cooperate if asked to perform a new duty), and outright opposition and resistance (either overt or covert). Eighty percent of employees tend to fall into the cooperative camp (support or acceptance) and twenty percent into the resistance camp.

Management staff's response to these camps is crucial to a successful change process. Management tends to be disturbed with the twenty percent and agonizes over how to move these individuals into the cooperative camp, or out of the agency. Change-based strategies are usually crafted with the twenty percent in mind. Communication vehicles (newsletters, memos, staff meetings, etc.), training events, and action plans are formed with a focus on the twenty percent. There are at least two problems with this approach:

1.   The twenty percent will largely not be persuaded by management's actions. The reasons for the resistance will be varied and complex. Some may not trust the change due to previous experiences. Some have not been convinced there is a compelling need for change. Some are experiencing major personal difficulties and cannot absorb any more change. Yet others are just predisposed to resist, as it is in their very nature. If they are open to change at all, it will be because of peer influence.

2.   The eighty percent will be trying to cooperate with their leaders but in so doing, will be taking some risks. They will be attempting to act or think differently, which they are not accustomed to doing. As a result, they are in need of additional support, reassurance, and encouragement. When management focuses on the twenty percent, the eighty percent is neglected. Worse, since management's messages are crafted with the 20% in mind, they may feel as though the leadership's message is critical of them or the overall lack of progress.

When management takes care of the eighty percent, the rest will either eventually follow, or their performance will not line up with the new agency values and expectations and they will leave the organization (by choice or force). Take the time to thank, recognize, and praise the employees who are cooperating and ask yourself how they can be fully supported. And give the eighty-percent reason to believe that they are exceptional and on the top of the bell curve.

?????? Challenge Question

Is the majority of attention toward change focused on the eighty percent of personnel who have accepted the change?

"*Good is not good enough.   Good is the enemy of great.*"

LEADERS AS PUSHERS

DISNEY IS ONE OF THE MOST VIBRANT AND SUCCESSFUL COMPANIES. In a recent annual report, they reported their revenues at 19 billion dollars! Revenues and profits have steadily risen year after year. Disney is a highly creative organization that churns out new, innovative products time and time again. In the 1996 annual report, CEO Michael Eisner ruminates in a sort of mid-life contemplative sort of way. And then he says something critically important. He discloses how he spends most of his day, every day. He reveals what he sees as the most important role for him to play in a premier, first-class company. He spends most of his time and thought process on how to develop and maintain the Disney culture! That's it! It's not pouring over spread-sheets, or negotiating new deals, or tweaking innovative concepts. As the CEO and leader of the Disney Corporation, he prioritizes his limited and therefore precious time on organizational culture issues.

What does this mean? As a leader, you are the keeper of the company values. You are the model for those values. Your actions are scrutinized even more than your words. Each little agency twist or turn is embodied in a reflection on the values to which the company adheres. When the existing employee actions don't line up with the desired culture, the CEO and the rest of the management staff must not overlook it. Instead, it must be identified as an action that threatens the vibrancy of the agency and needs changing. This embodies the constant, vigilant act of shaping corporate culture.

Leaders are really pushers. They are diligent in knowing and articulating the agency's values, and in ensuring that the agency behavior lines up with those values. That means that they have to be prepared to push people past their comfort zone. This is not for the squeamish. If a manager is a people-pleaser, it will be excruciatingly difficult for him/her to fill the role of pusher.

This doesn't imply that leaders shouldn't listen or be willing to change their point of view. Listening is even more important. Why isn't the change taking place? What are the real reasons? Is there something inherently wrong with the chosen course of action? What barriers exist which leadership can eliminate so the agency can reach the vision? At the same time, leadership needs to be aware that resistance is to be expected and that some degree of pushing will be necessary to make progress. This pushing will create discomfort and possible conflict, but it is a necessary part of the growth process. Leaders must be willing to put themselves in that position.

????? Challenge Question

Do the leaders model agency values and help push the agency closer to those values?

"Stability has become the enemy of survival."
— Steven Rhinamit
"Training and Development,"
March 1992

THE VALUE OF PANIC

MAYBE IT'S NORMAL THAT WE ACT THIS WAY. We wait to bring the family car in for a tune-up only after something breaks down. We don't lose weight or stop smoking until we reach a health crisis. We linger in the sun past the time when we know we will get sunburned. Whether it is human nature, procrastination, or complacency, it is commonplace—and this trait is also evident in the workplace. Expressed and unexpressed words seemingly are whispered, and sometimes shouted, everwhere: "Why change?" "What's broken?" "Things are fine now." "It's not that bad." "Why now?"

Due to the anxiety created by change, some level of resistance is natural even when the employee accepts the reasoning. Our equilibrium is threatened. Control over our life's events is at risk. In many cases, we expend more energy opposing or avoiding the change than if we would just accept it and adapt to it.

An immovable object requires a quick, short burst of energy to get it moving. Perhaps nothing works better than a sense of panic, much like how complacency is shattered when a hostile foreign country mobilizes the minds, energies, and resources of a whole nation. When an organization is not getting the job done, it may need a real or perceived crisis. It is during these times of panic that we reach deep down and accomplish things of which we didn't think we were capable. Sometimes a CEO needs to articulate the state of affairs in a forthright but compelling manner, which illuminates the urgency of the moment. We do not need to create artificial threats, as the enemies of our success are real and always present. They just need to be painted clearly and with ominous faces. There is no room for foot-dragging or complacency in a time of crisis; rather, it demands action by all.

Challenge Question

Does the leadership create a sense of urgency when too much inertia is prohibiting motivation for change?

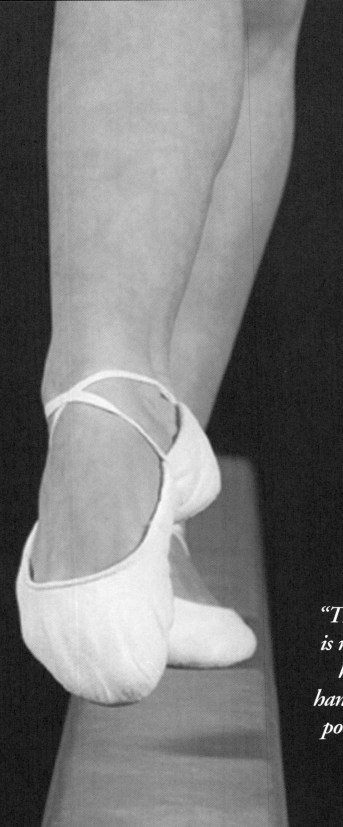

*"The game of life
is not so much in
holding a good
hand as playing a
poor hand well."*
H.T. Leslie

THE SHIFT-AND-BALANCE DANCE

JUGGLING THE MULTITUDE OF PRIORITIES WITH LIMITED RESOURCES feels like walking a balance beam in gymnastics. Leaning the wrong way can cause a painful fall. When an agency sets its course in a different direction, it causes a shift of resources and priorities. That's a scary proposition when the balance beam is narrow!

Yet, it is precisely this shift of resources that is required of the leadership. A major change effort will require altered priorities and practices. Such shifts will not win management any popularity contest. It will mean that someone's budget or project will be altered or even eliminated as another priority is elevated.

This is a test of administration's courage. Is the leadership willing to make the hard decisions about shifting priorities, or is it going to get watered down in a process riddled with compromise and turf protection?

An unintentional message during this time is that the activities conducted by employees up to the change moment were not valuable, that they have not been engaging in a meaningful work process. This is a false but natural conclusion. When you enter a museum, you will see outdated equipment such as the coal locomotive engine, horse carriage, or wooden washboards. All of these tools served a valuable and useful purpose in their time. But as new, more efficient replacements were invented or discovered, these tools were replaced. The objective, therefore, should be to celebrate the retired role of these tools used by the agency as we prepare to welcome the new.

Challenge Question

Is the leadership willing to shift agency resources to reinforce a new direction even when widely criticized for it?

DEVELOPING AND SUSTAINING A DYNAMIC, CREATIVE ORGANIZATION

"God gave us two ears but only one mouth. Some people say that's because he wanted us to spend twice as much time listening as talking. Others claim it's because he knew listening was twice as hard as talking."

MEAT-AND-
POTATOES RULE

ORGANIZATIONS OFFER A WIDE ARRAY OF SERVICES AND PRODUCTS. Issues are constantly bombarding leadership. Production costs, distribution problems, encroaching competition, a new opportunity, union conflicts, staff morale, space constraints, etc.—all such issues may be internal or external to the core agency mission. Yet, they constantly compete for limited time and attention of agency leadership. It is precisely due to the scope of this buffet of issues, that the ingestion of meat and potatoes gets overlooked.

What comprises the "meat and potatoes" of any organization? It is the customer. How well has the agency defined the customer? Once defined, how well does the agency cater to the customer's needs and wishes? Is the agency's attention diverted from its core mission?

The most successful companies have figured this out. They will not tolerate any arrogance or ignorance in this area. Not listening or responding to customers is grounds for termination. It's that important. In fact, they make their customers the number one priority. They trip over each other in an attempt to listen to the customer and meet a need. It doesn't mean that the feedback is always acted on, or done exactly in the manner as proposed by the customer. But all of this information gets stored even if not acted on immediately. The agency recognizes that they would not exist if it were not for the customer. It's gross in its simplicity. Yet, the buffet of issues is constantly tugging at it, pulling the agency into an internal focus. Once looking inward, the customers cannot be seen.

How often are your customers surveyed, formally or informally? How often do you spontaneously sit down next to someone in your waiting room and ask how your company is doing, and what you could help them with? Are you willing to listen, really listen, beyond the politeness to hear the discontent? Do you probe, or just leave when you hear what you hoped to hear?

Challenge Question

Are the customers given utmost attention as demonstrated by listening to them, conducting surveys, being responsive, etc.?

"Babe Ruth, perhaps the greatest player t o ever play professional baseball, hit 714 home runs, second only to Hank Aaron. But he also struck out 1,330 times."

"The average millionaire entrepreneur has filed for bankruptcy an average of 3.75 times!"

"With the number of pilots we've been involved in, we should have started an airline."

Dave Rooney

"Failure isn't falling down. It's staying down."

FAIL NOT,
SUCCEED NOT

SUCCESS DOES NOT COME CHEAPLY, OR WITHOUT PAIN. Success is a close relative of failure. Most of the better companies understand this, but how to respond to failure is difficult, particularly when the costs for the failure are severe or when mistakes are repeated.

There is a difference between taking a risk and taking a chance. Unlike chance, risks are calculated. A decision is made even when all of the consequences cannot be anticipated. One way to limit the fallout from unknown negative consequences, is to conduct pilot projects. Pilots allow an agency to try out new ideas, products, and practices without risking large-scale cost or loss of image or personnel.

A creative organization must expect failure. Failure is inherent within the definition of creativity. One cannot break new ground without turning up unexpected stones. Are only successes celebrated? Shouldn't we also celebrate those things at which we fail if they were risks and not chances? Don't we always gain some knowledge from failure? How much is that knowledge worth to the agency?

Do you think winners think much about losing? No, they have an expectancy about them. They focus on the end sight. They visualize the victory at the end of the road. They are not paralyzed by fear of failure. They do not allow negative thinking to cloud the dream. That is not to say that obstacles and concerns are ignored. Instead, they are attacked with vigor. The difference is that they do not allow inevitable setbacks to create despondency and surrender. They are just new challenges to overcome which make the eventual success all the much more satisfying. And if failure should happen to occur, winners use it as a learning tool. The focus is always on the prize.

Challenge Question

Does the agency value those lessons learned from failure, and expect that their employees will risk?

"*A mind once stretched by a new idea, never regains its original dimensions.*"

– Author unknown

DON'T
NEGOTIATE
WITH
LEPRECHAUNS

GREAT IDEAS ARE LIKE COMETS. They come our way every few dozen years. So, they should be treated as they are—extremely special and unique. They need to be treasured and protected as something rare and precious. Managers and leaders are keepers of ideas' survival. Leaders provide the substance that will either nurture that idea or starve it. It doesn't matter how it dies, whether the manager takes some action to poison it, or whether it withers from neglect. The result is the same. The moment of breakthrough has come and gone, and the company has nothing to show for it, except a frustrated innovator and a lost opportunity.

Great ideas are like discovering gold at the end of a rainbow. You know the folklore. If you can somehow reach the end of the rainbow before it dissipates, the pot of gold waiting for you is yours to keep. It is a treasure so rare and incredible, words cannot describe it. The small, roguish elf, however, is the protector of pots of gold. The leprechaun is the owner of many crocks of treasure. This elf must give up the pot of gold unless he can trick you into taking your eyes off him. Of course, he is full of treachery and will do whatever it takes to avoid having to give up the gold. Somehow, the leprechaun, in Irish folklore, is able to engage in sparring conversation, negotiations, trickery, and other forms of diversion, so that few if any humans have ever walked way with treasure. They succeed in diverting our eyes from the prize. Would you negotiate with a leprechaun under those conditions? When an idea so powerful comes your way, you may only have one chance to channel its potential. This is not the time to compromise or water down its poignancy. It must be retained in its full potency.

All too often, innovators watch their ideas slowly get dismantled. Usually, the reasons are shrouded in something called practicality. Upon closer examination, however, practicality means it would require a change in how we produce our services or products, as if such processes are unshakable givens. Agency leaders need to be protectors of the ideas, as if they were guarding a pot of gold. The leprechauns must be chased away.

There are plenty of ideas that can be tweaked and negotiated to minimize agency disruption and still get the job done. You will know them when you see them. The question is whether you will have the fortitude to protect them against organizational cannibalism. These "pot of gold" ideas are so significantly valuable that any compromise is too costly. Many examples in our history come to mind: color television, microwaves, the light bulb, computers, etc. Can you imagine what it would be like if Thomas Edison had allowed his concept of a light bulb to be compromised and watered down to a candle?

Challenge Question

Are unique, groundbreaking innovations compromised, or are they vigorously supported?

"We are what we repeatedly do. Excellence, then, is not
an act, but a habit."

– Aristotle

"We drill more wells."

– Amoco
(explaining why they
are the top U.S. company in finding oil)

CALL ON KOUBA

My brother-in-law Bill taught me a valuable lesson. In the coming year, it was to be my in-laws' 40th wedding anniversary. They are wonderful, giving people, and my brother-in-law wanted to make it a special event. He was in an art gallery when the idea struck him. His family had an old farmstead in North Dakota, which has withstood many generations of droughts, the depression, escalating farm prices, and an occasional bumper crop. The piece of property embodied the family history and, in many ways, the history of the American farmer. Les Kouba is an internationally known wildlife artist. His paintings are sought after both as quality art pieces as well as for investors who collect limited editions. Bill approached Kouba and requested that he paint the family homestead. After a few photo exchanges and a description of the family history, Kouba agreed. He finished the work the following season and sold the piece entitled "Old Home Reunion" in art galleries across the country. Each family member has a print with an original waterproof.

How many of us would have acted on that impulsive thought? By doing so, Bill has established a special sense of pride in each family member for generations to come. We all have these beyond-our-reach ideas but we talk ourselves out of them, or allow others to squelch our dreams. Opportunities are rarely convenient. They require action, usually quick action—before we change our minds.

The phrase of "Just Do It" has been plastered all over our television and printed advertising. Many corporations have expressed its virtues. "Just Do It" demands an action orientation. It suggests the use of experimentation and pilots as a way to risk without putting a lot of resources on the line.

Despite the widespread popularization of the phrase and the concept it embodies, little has changed in a multitude of agencies. The reasons are many: paralysis by analysis, fear of failure, intolerance for mistakes or risks, overcautious boards or CEOs, bureaucratic sterilization, etc. Once again, it is an organizational culture, which dictates whether a bias for action exists.

It's not really surprising. Our culture is bombarded with negative messages and intolerance for imperfection. The media seems to dwell on the glasses being half empty rather than half full. Even our language suggest that we err on the safe side: "better safe than sorry," "go slow," "easy does it," "don't get too big for your britches," etc.

I once heard some advice from my friend's mother. She said, "If you are looking for someone to help you get something done, find someone who is too busy." Busy people find ways to get things done. They don't overthink things. That doesn't mean they are knee-jerkers either. Taking action without forethought actually takes more time—that is, more time to fix what went wrong and to redo it. These are people who don't wait for an opportunity to come to them, they create opportunities. They don't wait till it's convenient to make a personal contact, they just pick up the phone. These are action-oriented people. To the outsider, it seems as if they get things done in their sleep. In a sense, they do. They start a number of other people thinking and doing things which eventually become finished products. Find people in your organization that enjoy action, and delegate.

Sometimes acting before we are convinced of the value of the change will create the attitude shift later. It is the strategy of changing attitudes by creating a willingness to try new behaviors. It is the willingness to try which is the precursor to a modification of our mindset. It is amazing how much resistance there can be to new ideas, and even more amazing how resistance can dissipate if the idea is just given a chance by putting it into action. We tend to believe in whatever actions we perform.

Challenge Question

Does the agency have a predisposition toward action, does it conduct pilots, and does it avoid overanalyzing ideas?

69

"The difference between a weed and a flower is a judgement."

THROW A PARTY

WHO CAN RESIST A GOOD PARTY?!? It's a great diversion from what appears to be our national pastime—finding what's wrong with everything and complaining about it. It's not just the media or politicians who point out what's wrong. We all do it. When we look at our aging face in the mirror, we dwell on the one or two gray hairs instead of the abundance of others. When our kids bring home a stellar report card, we ignore all the A's and ask about the A minus. When we bring home a pay raise and a great performance review, we dwell on the one passing comment on how we could improve future performance. The stress we feel today is largely self-induced.

A business personality is not unlike that of an individual. It also tends to be overrun with complaining. This is different than never being satisfied. A lack of final satisfaction can be healthy and lead to continuous quality improvement. Having a complaint disposition as an agency means that collectively there exists an atmosphere of discontentment and negativism. That negative energy diverts the agency from focusing on its vision, it squashes creativity, and it causes the agency to be internally focused, away from its customers. The solution is to throw a party!

As important as celebration events are, they cannot take the place of a daily atmosphere of appreciation and celebration. It must be a process as opposed to an event. To act in a festive manner one day out of the year will appear artificial and insincere if it isn't reinforced by a similar, ongoing organization attitude.

Celebrating our successes, even minor ones, helps us tap into our optimism and pride. When employees are proud of where they work, and are excited about where the agency is headed, they are focused on how they can contribute. It is a festive mindset. When our minds are engaged and we view the company as our own, we tap into our most creative selves.

How do you celebrate your successes? Do you make a big deal about those things that are core to your mission, or does it look as though you take them for granted? How proud are your employees about the company and its product? Do they feel as though they personally helped create the agency and are committed to its continued success?

Challenge Question

Does the agency go out of its way to celebrate successes, even small ones?

71

"With the help of an "if" you might put Paris in a bottle."
– French Proverb

FEEDING THE
PRAYING MANTIS

THE PRAYING MANTIS PROJECTS A POWERFUL IMAGE FOR US. After sharing an intimate moment, the female mantis proceeds to bite the head off the male. To an outside observer, it appears to be a self-destructive act for the entire mantis species. One cannot imagine modeling behavior after its ritual. Yet, it is precisely this activity that marks so many organizations.

Who or what is the greatest threat to an organization? What is the greatest stifler of ideas, particularly those ideas with the potential to lead an organization to a new level of performance? Are these threats internal or external to the agency? More often than not, the detracting forces tend to come from the very individuals within the organization who have contributed so much to its current success.

Organizations are characterized by status quo forces. New ideas and change initiatives threaten equilibrium. What is the common result? Organizational cannibalism or the tendency to consume the very source of new ideas and basis for action. Threats come in may forms: "We can't do that." "That won't work because…" "It is too costly." Compare these responses to "How can we make this happen?" "What would it take to do this?"

We tend to envision the "thirty-foot wall of burning oil" and think of all sorts of reasons why or how we would get burned if we tried to scale it. In other words, we become paralyzed with fear and negativity. We spend an inordinate amount of time processing the "why's and why not's." The net result is that the organization eats away at its very creative self. Is it any wonder we become frustrated with the lack of progress? That is why so many consultants advise blowing something up and starting from scratch instead of working with an existing culture.

We all don't have the luxury of blowing something up. So we have at least two other options—move decisively or feed the mantis.

1.   Move decisively means that once you become aware that you cannot overcome or contain the resistance in a timely fashion, you move with blazing speed and razor-sharp decisiveness. You implement the change once you have entered the theater of ideas. You do not waste any energy or resources on unwinnable battles. And you always, always keep your aim on the final target. This can be a good strategy. Of course, the danger is (as we know from the chapter on buy-in ratio) is that the rest of the organization may not line up and implement the changes to the degree necessary. This leaves you with Option 2.

2.   Feed the mantis. An organization that cannibalizes its best ideas is doing it for a reason. It may be that too much competition exists among employees. It may be an overload of change, rendering employees with a lack of ability to absorb any more change. It could be the creation of a culture of naysaying. It could even simply be a lack of training. The agency is acting a certain way for a reason. By finding out the reasons(s), you can offer alternative ways of getting that need met.

With either option, the leadership must be very clear on how it feels about killing ideas. Citing reasons that something can't work may be instructive, but the emphasis on "can't" or "won't" takes the agency out of the game altogether.

????? Challenge Question

Is there an agency expectation around innovation that demands a "how to" versus a "can't do" approach?

"*Even if you're on the right track, you'll get run over if you just sit there.*"
— Will Rogers

APPENDIX

Change Readiness Disposition Assessment

The following self-assessment is designed to help you determine if your organization is ready for systemic, cultural change; prepared to apply techniques that take into account the costs of change; cognizant of employee needs; and ready to take on leadership functions. This assessment is designed to be conducted quickly, and to serve as a tool for preparing your management team and helping to identify gaps in your strategic action plan.

	Strongly Agree	Agree	Neither Agree or Disagree	Disagree	Strongly Disagree
1. The agency recognizes that employee motives differ, and provides individual approaches to institute changes.	+2	+1	0	-1	-2
2. Opportunities are given for employees to get their basic needs met (security, belonging, competence, self-fulfillment, curiosity, etc.)	+2	+1	0	-1	-2
3. Employees are given regular opportunities to shape most major agency decisions.	+2	+1	0	-1	-2
4. Desired employee behavior is recognized and acknowledged in small ways on a day-to-day basis.	+2	+1	0	-1	-2
5. Individual employees are recognized for their accomplishments in the presence of their peers.	+2	+1	0	-1	-2
6. Work is a fun place to be.	+2	+1	0	-1	-2
7. Eccentric, creative mavericks are supported and protected by management.	+2	+1	0	-1	-2
8. Major change processes start with efforts that are a guaranteed success.	+2	+1	0	-1	-2
9. Respected figures are recruited for support of major change events.	+2	+1	0	-1	-2
10. Employees' reward mechanisms line up with new, desired agency directions.	+2	+1	0	-1	-2
11. Significant effort is placed on hiring and molding new employees whose attributes and traits are consistent with the new agency vision.	+2	+1	0	-1	-2

12. Employees, stakeholders, and customers are given more time to adapt to those ideas which are more threatening.	+2	+1	0	-1	-2
13. Outcome measures clearly line up with desired agency direction, and are visible to all responsible for the outcomes.	+2	+1	0	-1	-2
14. The agency has stories and symbols which powerfully communicate the company's purpose and the expectations of all personnel.	+2	+1	0	-1	-2
15. Leadership has long-lasting stamina to outlast existing remnants of culture that resist change.	+2	+1	0	-1	-2
16. Leadership understands the art of channeling energy rather than directly fighting it.	+2	+1	0	-1	-2
17. Leadership is conscious of little, spontaneous ways in which they communicate messages to employees.	+2	+1	0	-1	-2
18. The agency consciously seeks to hire flexible personnel.	+2	+1	0	-1	-2
19. The agency vision is communicated in ways that enable employees to imagine what it will look like when reached.	+2	+1	0	-1	-2
20. The majority of attention toward change is focused on the 80% of personnel who have accepted the change.	+2	+1	0	-1	-2
21. Leaders model agency values and help push the agency closer to those values.	+2	+1	0	-1	-2
22. Leadership creates a sense of urgency when too much inertia is prohibiting motivation for change.	+2	+1	0	-1	-2
23. Leadership is willing to shift agency resources to reinforce a new direction even when widely criticized for it.	+2	+1	0	-1	-2
24. The customers are given utmost attention as demonstrated by listening to them, conducting surveys, being responsive, etc.	+2	+1	0	-1	-2

25. The agency values those lessons learned from failure, and expects that their employees will risk.	+2	+1	0	-1	-2
26. Unique, groundbreaking innovations are not compromised, but are vigorously supported.	+2	+1	0	-1	-2
27. The agency has a predisposition toward action, conducts pilots, and avoids overanalyzing ideas.	+2	+1	0	-1	-2
28. The agency goes out of its way to celebrate successes, even small ones.	+2	+1	0	-1	-2
29. There is an agency expectation around innovation that demands a "how to" versus a "can't do" approach.	+2	+1	0	-1	-2

KEY

Over 25	You are thriving.
12 to 24	Good. Some improvement needed.
0 to 11	Significant improvement needed.
Less than 0	Go on a retreat.

ABOUT THE AUTHOR

Mark Carey is the Deputy Commissioner of the Community and Juvenile Services Division in the Minnesota Department of Corrections. Previously he was the Director of Community Corrections in Dakota County, Minnesota. The Community Corrections Department is responsible for supervision and programming for juvenile and adult offenders either sentenced by the court to probation or released from prison and state institutions. Mr. Carey has a Bachelor's Degree from Moorhead State University in Criminal Justice and has over twenty years of experience as a counselor, probation officer, college instructor, trainer, planner, and administrator. He has his own consulting business, Carey Enterprises. Mr. Carey is a nationally renowned speaker, writer, and consultant on restorative justice and other criminal justice areas. He has been recognized nationally for his work, and much of his writing has been published and widely distributed. He lives in Lakeville, Minnesota, with his wife and two children.